SELECTED POEMS 1942-1972

By the same author

POETRY
The Enemies of Love
Hurlygush
At the Wood's Edge
Ode for St. Andrew's Night and Other Poems
The Exiled Heart
Snow Warning
One Later Day
This Business of Living
Comings and Goings

PROSE
The Lowlands of Scotland: Glasgow and the North
The Lowlands of Scotland: Edinburgh and the South
The Scottish Renaissance
Robert Burns: the Man: his Work: the Legend
The Burns Encyclopedia
Clyde Waters
By Yon Bonnie Banks
The Discovery of Scotland: Travellers in Scotland from the thirteenth to the eighteenth centuries
Environment: a Basic Human Right
The Eye is Delighted: Some Romantic Travellers in Scotland
Portrait of Glasgow

ANTHOLOGIES
Poetry Scotland 1-4 (4 with Hugh MacDiarmid)
No Scottish Twilight (with Fred Urquhart)
Modern Scottish Poetry: an Anthology of the Scottish Renaissance
John Davidson: Selected Poems: with a preface by T. S. Eliot and an introduction by Hugh MacDiarmid
A Book of Scottish Verse (World Classics)
Scottish Poetry 1-6 (with George Bruce and Edwin Morgan)

MAURICE LINDSAY

SELECTED POEMS

1942-1972

ROBERT HALE & COMPANY

© Maurice Lindsay 1973
First published in Great Britain 1973

ISBN 0 7091 4000 2

Robert Hale & Company
63 Old Brompton Road
London S.W.7.

*Published with the support of the
Scottish Arts Council*

Printed in Great Britain by
Clarke, Doble & Brendon Ltd.
Plymouth

CONTENTS

PREFACE

Though the final choice was mine, I am grateful to the several friends and literary colleagues who have given me advice on the selection of these poems. They are placed in roughly chronological order. Many have been substantially revised since their first appearance.

M.L.

For Joyce
with love and gratitude

THE SUDDEN PICTURE
(for Joyce)

My days are stained with people, purposeless
and restless as the heart of this hurt city;
hopes geared like watches, darted troutlike fears,
and the exquisite paraphernalia of self-pity.

And walking in these white, half-frightened streets,
I remember you, leaning against a wind from the Tay;
the smile your eyes launched into loveliness
that drowned the careful words I meant to say.

I might have told you just the usual stories
each first new lover weaves into a name;
held you above the well-applauded glories,
or wrapped you in a personal dream of fame.

But I said nothing; for the sudden picture
you made against a light blown from the sea
mocked war's unnatural, accidental virtue
and meant far more than Stalingrad for me.

Now all the roads of Europe lead to horror,
time cannot heal Cassino's fountained stones;
beneath the gag of darkness, millions cower
in menaced, dingy, still unbattered homes.

They are gashed with the same guilt, friend and enemy,
a wound reeks round their striving circled years:
the future mirrors back reversed deceptions,
tomorrow floats on history's stale tears.

My darling, since the words I never uttered
were more than guns' mad gestures, more than death's
advances over towns that men have shattered,
I send you love, and with it all my faith.

JOCK, THE LAIRD'S BROTHER

Strutting across the red moors of his memory, Jock, the Laird's
    brother,
tingling, tweedy bagpipe trousers, whisky map-veined face,
under his arm a leering gun, the image of his father,
the skirling tradition of fishes and pheasants, the ownership of
    space;

the purple, peopleless moors of Scotland where poverty seeds in
    the ground,
and love turns grey as the ashy, prickled, bleak-burned skele-
    toned heather,
where sleek guns splutter their patter in August, and gasping
    grouse are found
on the noses of snuffling dogs, and the hills are always the talk
    of weather.

Once, he was keeper of animals claimed from God to be owned
    by a Scottish lord;
once, he patrolled the edges of forests, a poacher's pleasure his
    full despair;
now, he is grown the villagers' measure with his regular walks,
    an old man, absurd,
with the look of one who was left behind by his thoughts, and
    is never here.

CELIA, THE WIFE O' THE LAIRD

Mrs. Mackintosh, wi heather-mixture suit,
hauds oot frae Brechin in a black coupé;
wi gloweran een, she gies the horn a toot
an scatters sheep an fairmers frae her way.

Wi graceful ease she purrs alang the road,
jinkan roun corners, shearan aff the hedge,
content wi smeddum that gat her sic a load
o meat, gin, whisky an cigarettes for Reg.

Aside her, Pooh, her Pomeranian dug,
snuffles the air, an stoiters roun the seat,
syne stretches oot upon the tartan rug
wi twitchan nose fowr inches frae the meat.

Dung-clortit fields flee past her like a flick.
Charming, she thinks, the Scottish Rural Scene.
Wi artfu glances Pooh begins tae lick
the paper whaur a pund o mince had been.

A line o cedars sweepan up a lawn,
an och! at last the weary journey's done.
The heather-mixture's crinkl't sit-upon
gets oot an stretches like a yeastful bun.

Wi green plus-fowrs and cheery Oxford cry,
dear Reg, the laird, comes doun tae greet his wife.
Anither week the warld can whidder by:
thae twa're bielded frae the blasts o life.

THE EXILED HEART

Two purple pigeons circle a London square
as darkness blurs and smudges the shadowless light
of a winter evening. I pause on the pavement and stare
at the restless flutter of wings as they gather flight,
like rustling silk, and move out to meet the night.

And my restless thoughts migrate to a Northern city—
fat pigeons stalking the dirty cobbled quays,
where a sluggish river carries the cold self-pity
of those for whom life has never flowed with ease,
from a granite bridge to the green Atlantic seas:

the bristling, rough-haired texture of Scottish manners;
the jostling clatter of crowded shopping streets
where lumbering tramcars squeal as they take sharp corners:
the boosy smell from lounging pubs that cheats
the penniless drunkard's thirst with its stale deceits:

where my heart first jigged to the harsh and steady sorrow
of those for whom mostly the world is seldom glad,
who are dogged by the flat-heeled, footpad steps of tomorrow;
for whom hope is a dangerous drug, an expensive fad
of the distant rich, or the young and lovesick mad:

where chattering women in tearooms, swaddled with furs,
pass knife-edged gossip like cakes, and another's skirt
is unstitched with sharp words, and delicate, ladylike slurs
are slashed on the not-quite-nice or the over-smart
till smoke to the eyes is a hazy, prickled hurt.

I remember Glasgow, where sordid and trivial breed
from the same indifferent father; his children side
with the mother whose sour breasts taught them first to feed
on her hot, caressing hates that sear and divide,
or swell the itching, distended bladder of pride.

12

Yet my guilty sneers are the tossed-down, beggar's penny
which the goaded heart throws out, in vain, to procure
the comfortable forgetfulness of the many
who lie in content's soft arms, and are safe and sure
in the fabled Grecian wanderers' lotus-lure;

who forget the sullen glare of the wet, grey skies,
and the lashing Northern wind that flicks the skin
like a whip, where poverty's dull and listless eyes
are pressed to the window, hearing the friendly din
of the party, watching the lights and laughter within.

But oh, I cannot forget, so I wait and wonder,
how long will the thinly dividing window hold,
how long will the dancing drown the terrible anger
of those, the unwanted, who peddle their grief in the cold,
wrapped in their own despair's thick and unkindly fold?

Yet evil is no pattern of places
varied, like terraces from town to town.
A city's charms and individual graces
are but the sculptor's bleak and basic stone,
the photographic face without a frown.

The wound is in this bewildered generation,
tossed on the swollen, analytic mood,
its compasspoint no longer veneration
of that lost God who rewarded the simple and good,
vivid and real, now, only in childhood.

For we, the children of this uncertain age,
breathing its huge disasters and sad airs,
have seen that our warm, humanitarian rage
is impotent to soothe war's animal fears,
can never quell the lonely exile's tears.

So the heart, like a wounded seabird, hungers home
to muffled memories on faintly-beating wings
which once climbed over history's clouded foam
to that clear sky where each new hero flings
the careful stone that fades in slow, concentric rings.

ON SEEING A PICTURE O' JOHANN CHRISTIAN FISCHER IN THE NATIONAL GALLERY, EDINBURGH

Johann Christian Fischer? Mm—the face is kindly,
the wig weil-snod, the features firmly set,
as leanan on a harpsichord by Kirkman
wi quill in haun you scrieve a menuet.

The feet sae carefully crossed tae shaw the buckl't shuin,
gimp hose and curly cravat o white lace,
the fiddle on the chair, the music heaped—
the hail, a glisk o 18th Century grace!

Gin ony o your stately airs and tunefu' dances
that kittl't pouther't duchesses lang syne,
culd tinkle oot o Kirkman's yella keyboard,
maist folk 'ud luk at you a second time.

But aa is dusty silence, like the derk ahint you,
and e'en your notes are naethin but a blur;
the background, fu o shaddaws, seems tae draw you
tae hap you in its aa-embracin slur.

Yet there you staun oot still, by Gainsborough made immortal,
as gin sic fame was shairly jist your due—
a perfect shell upon the shore left strandit,
a piece for antiquarians tae view.

J. C. Fischer (1733–1800) was a German oboeist and composer, born in
Freiburg, who first visited London in 1768 and spent much of his time
there. He was friendly with J. C. Bach. Fischer married the daughter of
Gainsborough, who painted the portrait that gave rise to this poem.

AT JOHN GALT'S GRAVE, GREENOCK
A living man upon a deid man thinks
HUGH MACDIARMID

The hills, the sunshine and the shadows meet
on this lown grave, abune a smokey toun,
whaur hap't wi thochts o your prood Scottish virr,
a livan wi a deid hert would commune.

Nae claggie earth nor gawpen wecht o stane
can come atween your eident saul and mine,
for through the years grown owre you, still I share
the things that maittered maist tae you, lang syne—

your luve o pawky carles, slee lawyer chiels,
braw leddies, strappin loons and saucy jauds:
your preean o their nervous Lallan tongue,
and aa the sklentan glisks its music hauds!

But suddenly oor silence faas apairt—
shrill shipyaird whussles blaw and hooters wail;
and oot intae the narrow, clorty streets
a hunner thoosan jostlan workers skail

wha've never heard o you, asleep up here,
wha, gin they kent your pouer, wuldna care
for ony o the lithe and subtle straiks
you used tae lay the Scottish psyche bare.

And I, as faur removed frae them as you,
dour, wycelike figure, are frae me, begin
tae feel thon airn claith o laneliness
you wore aboot you like a second skin.

HURLYGUSH

The hurlygush and hallyoch o the watter
skinklan i the moveless simmer sun
harles aff the scaurie mountain wi a yatter
that thru ten-thoosan centuries has run.

Wi cheek against the ash o wither't bracken
I ligg at peace and hear nae soun at aa
but yonder hurlygush that canna slacken
thru time and space mak never-endan faa:

as if a volley o the soun had brocht me
doun tae the pool whaur timeless things begin,
and e'en this endless faa'in that had claucht me
wi ilka ither force was gether't in.

Hurlygush: the sound of running water
hallyoch: the noise made by water on stones
harles: peels

LILY-LOWE

O orange tiger-lily, burnan bricht,
swung lantern at the end o the sun's licht,
your caunel-stamens' drippan yalla ase
dazzles the bummers wi its dusty haze;

and your silk petals' incandescent flare,
like hot, fresh wax, sae mells wi the deep air
o hinnied Simmer, that I canna tell
jist whaur the blue lift rings the rim o your bell.

FAINT-HERT
(frae the 12th Century Erse)

Douce bell, dulce bell,
   strucken against this wind-blawn nicht,
I'd liefer be keepan tryst wi you
   nor a flichterie woman, faus and licht!

AGAINST THE BLASTING OF TRUMPETS

John Knox, old thumping beard-and-testament master,
who found God's word a thunder-splitting roar
that chafed far more than the sweat-smoothed buck of the oar
you levered through the splashed and lashed disaster
that sucked your middle years; up from the galleys
you brought salt's burning and the parch of seas,
a chain-ribbed, fiery conscience; and with these
to rub your ire, you rabbled bumpkin rallies
of fanatic peasants, hurt with feudal wrongs,
word-battering till you rang their hearts like gongs.

Most venerable ranting, randy preacher,
women you thought no bible-staining sin;
wedded, they stilled the beast's besetting din
that troubled even you, haranguing teacher

whose tongue bit under blood and germinated
its blind, corroding, parasitic kin—
Intolerance that breathed no difference in;
Power and Force that never need be sated
since God sat in your bowels, and through your beard
blew forth the single Trewth to be revered.

Deforming man who mocked the shape of wonder,
(your nightly arms lulled round a lass's waist)
who spat forth loveliness like some foul taste,
racked fugues and rendered soaring walls asunder;
usurping man, who stripped Christ's mythic story
of meek forgiveness, up from every land
you helped force loose the ultimate staying hand.
Popes, Calvins, Marxes share your shabby glory:
where men are tortured, riddled freedom falls,
hidden in hating hearts your monument tolls.

A VIEW OF LOCH LOMOND

Mountains open their hinged reflections on the loch,
shape and reshape themselves, grow squat or tall,
are bent by shakes of light. We never find
the same place twice; which is why picture postcards
that claim to lay the constant on the table
(the camera cannot lie) are popular;
from me to you, a reassuring fable;
what trotting tourists hoped to purchase for the shelf;
the image they'd retain, if they were able.

But landscape's an evasion of itself.

TRAVELLERS' TALES

The paddle-steamer pulls its own bent image
over loch water, through a rippling screen
that makes itself, tall mountains, trees and islands
            twisted and squat, and seem to lean
out of the shapes of what we think they mean.

Tourists, anonymous behind dark glasses,
admire the scene, yet feel that something's wrong,
they're not sure what; the wind's in the wrong quarter,
            the season's late, the sun's too strong,
the ship's too slow, or perhaps the loch's too long!

According to our childhood expectations
landscape should wear the look of history,
and island waters lap soft wordless legends.
            No place, wherever it may be,
preserves impersonal objectivity.

Which is why journeys usually disappoint us:
until we're there we always hope to find
escape from discontent, somehow forgetting
            the self we never leave behind
makes all we see half attitude of mind.

FARM WOMAN

She left the warmth of her body tucked round her man
before first light, for the byre, where mist and the moist
hot breath of the beasts half-hid the electric veins
of the milking machines. Later, she'd help to hoist

the heavy cans for the tractor to trundle down
to the farm-road end, while her raw hands scoured the dairy.
By seven o'clock, she'd have breakfast on the table,
her kitchen bright as her apron pin, the whole house airy.

Her men-folk out in the fields, the children off to school,
she'd busy herself with the house and the hens. No reasons
clouded the other side of the way she brought
to her man the generous amplitude of the seasons.

Not much of a life, they'd whisper at church soirées
as they watched her chat, her round face buttered with content,
unable to understand that for her each moment
rubbed out the one before, and simply lent
nothing for words of theirs to touch to argument.

BULL SHOW

Worn men in tweeds from the world's plains and valleys,
women whose breeding's wrapped in rugs and furs,
lounge by the ring where lurching, sweaty herdsmen
with faces that speak seasons, coax and curse
the curly little bulls, taming their paces
to haltered rounds on urine-stenching sand,
far from the trembling fields, the cows of challenge.

Brows marked with thought, marked catalogues in hand,
these well-worn men and well-bred women stare,
seeing, not blackness, curliness nor shape,
nor bull moustaches breathed on frosted air,
but bull that never was; all that a bull should be:
as perfect as their own reality.

WAITRESS

Shaken blowsily loose by the clatter of trays
and the doors that slap her bottom, armpits breathing,
she wipes herself on the table to dust at crumbs
that fly off, leaving sixpence beneath a cup,
rattles warm knives on clean-worn plates, and says
her ducks and dearies what-you-can have, half-seething
with weariness because nothing ever comes
between last fetch-and-carry and next wash-up.

What might have happened once, no man now cares
to think about, though surely she must have been pretty
enough not just to be left to wait
while the battered kitchen swing-doors flipped away
her youth. This patient, sweaty to-and-froing she wears
should earn her more than her wages, tipped with pity;
but living won't negotiate the rate
it'll take for the job, let alone how much it'll pay.

BARMAID

The drinks are served. The liquefaction of your clothes
settles, and strands you in a raddled de Milo pose
that shapes your girdled belly, sweatered breasts, glazed thighs
to quintessential woman. The bored and vacant eyes
of the men disguising themselves from themselves in the bar
focus on private images of you, a-spar
in the open routine of love. You're no longer what you are—
an ageing lay whom nobody thought worth keeping,
but the rawness of sex clammed succubously, raking
all generative masculinity.

21

Compulsive giving, they'd say, should have no affinity
with love; yet often, the drug of dutiful rapture spent,
they've turned on their pillows, wondering what myth had rent;
if dying could be different.

You pluck yourself at the rim of your bra's itch,
and you're shabbily what you were; a blethering good-humoured
    bitch,
never quite sure what's happening, or how men think . . .

One of them loudly calls for another drink.

ANY NIGHT IN THE VILLAGE PUB

Plodding in from the fields of his memory,
he'd shoulder the pub door open, scrape his boots
on the edge of their chatter, order his pint and chaser,
then stand propped there, a tree pulled up by the roots.

He never argued their odds, nor smirked when they told him
Jock had put Andra's lass in the family way.
When strangers led the talk to the state of the weather,
he'd grunt and glower, as if in his beer the answer lay.

Some said he'd broken his bairnless wife in bedded fury;
that he who mated beasts and seasons, had
no son from his own seed. Others discreetly hinted
living so long alone would drive any man to the bad.

All of them lowered their voices when he joined them,
aware of his self-sufficiency that hung
about the room till he banged down his angry money
and breenged back into the darkness from which he'd come,
leaving them, oddly disturbed, a whiff of carbolic and dung.

EPITAPH FOR A FARMER

Clumsily, like one of his own beasts
made purposeful, he moved through the mud of the steading,
taking no thought of his comfort, mashing his meals,
crumpling an unmade couch, though now and then bedding

some filly girl on the hayrick behind the shed
where the raw cock screeches the mist from each new morning.
Eleven o'clock, and the clatter of his tractor
gave gentle folk in the village shop due warning

to get their business finished, for he'd come in
stramping the cold, his cheek-bones the clouds' bruises,
his clothes steaming of sweat and dung, his strong breath
visible. Not one who gains or loses

at the toss of a season, they said, he racked his joyless days
like generations of his blood before him,
merely to make the earth articulate.
Honour his line; then, if you will, deplore him.

FARM WIDOW

She moved among the sour smell of her hens' droppings,
her cheeks rubbed to a polish, her skirts bustled
with decent pride; alone since the day the tractor
hauled itself up the field on the hill and toppled

her man away from her. Around her feet
her daughter played, the face of innocence puckered
with the solemn self-importance of being alone
in a grown-up world; her friends, the hens that speckled

her mother's allotment. Some of the weekly folk
who came to buy their eggs, watched her counting
their change from the money in her purse, and had given her
silent pity, then sensed that she wasn't wanting

anything they could offer; that she seemed
like one whom life had used too soon for writing
some sort of purpose with, her gestures' economies
spelling completeness; gone beyond our waiting

for times and places to happen, behind the will,
to where time and place lie colourless and still.

COUNTRY FUNERAL

Under vague humps you lie there, side by side,
who never in life could have endured one another;
wind and rain that once blew against you chide
forever from your tombs, and rough grasses smother

the shape of your each long rest that nobody shares.
Though the country steeple showers its cracked farewells
on mourned and mourners, between your world and ours
is only a different poverty: breath like the sound of the bells.

For you, too, must have felt the thrust of clouds
on your fields, the wrap and unwrap of storms
and as sudden calms; how sometimes a season crowds
itself so much as to make heroic harms.

Forgotten fathers who have done with proving
over again the insane geometries of chance,
encompassed by the easement of your loving
in an as lonely world where different words still glance

and clatter off the same evasions of meaning,
as the afternoon fades into its own dying
and tombs and new-turned earth begin to lose their seeming,
for you and all men dead and now our hearts are crying

wide with compassion who have none to give.
The black snows of darkness gather about the hills;
dust skitters the coffin; the mourners leave to live;
and with its old indifference the abandoned clay refills.

A FIFTEENTH-CENTURY ALTAR-PIECE

The rich old Roman for whose private solace
this Gothic Christ was windowed in fine gold,
shared with his peasants, who were Daddi's models,
a certainty the years seemed to uphold.

Such certainty, there was no need to question
the dragging body symbolled on its cross,
so never cause to learn that being certain
itself implies a kind of inverse loss.

The Roman prayed before his triptych, finding
in the clear centre consolation lay:
now, certainty uncentred, my gaze searches
those edges that in shadows fall away.

SEAGULLS

Seagulls coasted hoarse with spume
flexing a wing's-breadth of unease
from shrugged-off clouds; a heave of tiny
shoulders mimicking the sea's;

voice of the blaffering winds' edge
haloing fishermen as they stoop
to nets or boxes; white stones
dropping themselves; a feathered scoop

to rip the living water, clip
bread from hands, or seize scraps
of fading entrails patterned
in the smell of decay; white paps

puffed on bollards against the breeze's
huffing; or hunched like age on rocks;
or tossed in sudden, unfurled panic:
the singleness of their cry mocks

the syllables we shape as words;
for we can't make sounds that say
nothing of love or hate, only
uncalculating necessity.

AT HANS CHRISTIAN ANDERSEN'S BIRTHPLACE, ODENSE, DENMARK

Sunlight folds back pages of quiet shadows
against the whitewashed walls of his birthplace.
                    Tourists move
through crowded antiseptic rooms and ponder
what row after row of glass-cased papers ought to prove.

Somehow the long-nosed gangling boy who was only
at home in fairyland, has left no clues.
The tinder-box of Time we rub
answers us each the way we choose.

26

For kings have now no daughters left for prizes.
Swineherds must remain swineherds; and no spell
can make the good man prince; psychiatrists
have dredged up wonder from the wishing well.

The whole of his terrible, tiny world might be
dismissed as a beautiful madman's dream, but that each
of us knows
whenever we move out from the warmth of our loneliness
we may be wearing the Emperor's new clothes.

AGED FOUR

Alone beside himself, head-in-air
he wanders gently through a fading season,
almost for the last time aware
of how a moment feels, before the lesion

of growing into thought begin to hurt;
the falling burn turn into a complaint
it can't communicate; earth on the hands be dirt
that rubs a sudden scolding up; each feint

the wind boxes the trees with, trace a why
nobody answers; rain be more than wet;
clouds that unfold each other, shape a sky
forecasting portent. Head-in-air, and yet

reluctant to come in, he stands and bawls,
sensing from how much loss his mother calls.

SMALL BOY WRITING

My little son beside me shapes his letters,
a tremulous M, a not-quite-meeting O,
sticking them with his breath down careful pages,
        row on repeated row.

He'll heir the questions elder, self-styled betters
have jumbled from these same laborious signs,
and find what somehow answered for their ages
        has slipped between the lines:

their lingered creeds and dogmas, slackened fetters
no longer strong enough to hold the mind
back from its baffled necessary sieges,
        though nothing's there behind.

He'll find how little we are still their debtors,
their purposes unpurposed, doubts secured
without assurances, their faith's self-pledges,
        lonelinesses endured.

So may he learn resistance to go-getters
prospecting ends and absolutes; be content
to take delight's quick shapes and sudden edges
        as living's monument.

SCHOOL PRIZEGIVING

The voice rose out of his enormous paunch
reverberant with wisdom rounded there
since he had stood, a sliver of himself
with boys like these in some lost otherwise

innumerable platitudes away.
And yet, for all its width, the voice was small,
smooth-feathered still, cock-crested in success
that time had caponed, centre of the hall.

And as his little meanings strutted out
in preening words, the eager fledgling boys
who listened must have wondered if they too
might one day make the same wing-beating noise

to keep their courage up, their run of years
inexplicably fouled, their hopeful hastes
turned back upon themselves; each still so sure
he'd force his way beyond these middle wastes. . . .

And I, aware how satisfaction breaks
against its realisation, and how thick
the darkness gathers, caught myself, ashamed,
half-murmuring: *Their prizes, masters. Quick!*

PICKING APPLES

Apple time, and the trees brittle with fruit.
My children climb the bent, half-sapping branches
to where the apples, cheeked with the hectic flush
of Autumn, hang. The children bark their haunches

and lean on the edge of their balance. The apples are out
of reach; so they shake the tree. Through a tussle of leaves
    and laughter
the apples thud down; thud on the orchard grasses
in rounded, grave finality, each one after

the other dropping; the muffled sound of them dropping
like suddenly hearing the beats of one's own heart
falling away, as if shaken by some storm
as localised as this. Loading them into the cart,

the sweet smell of their bruises moist in the sun,
their skin's bloom tacky against the touch,
I experience fulfilment, suddenly aware
of some ripe, wordless answer, knowing no such

answers exist; only questions, questions, the beating years,
the dropped apples . . . the kind of touch and go
that poetry makes satisfaction of;
reality, with nothing more to show

than a brush of branches, time and the apples falling,
and shrill among the leaves, children impatiently calling.

A PICTURE OF THE CALEDONIAN HUNT

Over their fences with superb aplomb
these claret-blooded hunting gentry soar,
their leathering women, mistresshood confirmed
by hourglass stays, and half their years to pour

unquestioned dominance down, curbed in and held
above the silence of their last halloo,
kept from oblivion by the picture's edge
that scuffed their breathless quarry out of view.

Why did they ride to hounds? Some need to assert
the blood's uncertainty, their rulership

of field and ditch? Or, like the pounded fox,
hopeful they'd give their warmest fears the slip?

Or did they straddle stallions to exult
and stretch those instincts men and horses share,
the satisfaction straining thews and sinews
relax into the sense of use and wear?

Did movement threaten from behind scrubbed hedges,
the spring of winter coiled in frosted mould
mock at their privilege, or seem to trap them
nearer the thicket of their growing old?

Still they survive, these lonely, frozen gestures;
the life they leaped at and were ground to, thawed
beneath them, gone with all they thought they stood for.
Yet were they further from whatever flowed

as clarity around their consciousness,
wearing away what living seemed to mean,
but somehow never did, than we are who
catch half-familiar glimpses of it, seen

as landscape flowing from a plane is; clean
in its detachment, of itself complete?
What we are left with here are the blanched stains
imprinting lineaments of a defeat

not different from ours, but doubly separated:
by the unexplorable geography
of time, each of us on our island of it
misted about in our own difficulty.

AT THE MOUTH OF THE ARDYNE

The water rubs against itself,
glancing many faces at me.
One winces as the dropped fly
tears its tension. Then it heals.

Being torn doesn't matter.
The water just goes on saying
all that water has to say,
what the dead come back to.

Then a scar opens.
Something of water is ripped out,
a struggle with swung air.
I batter it on a loaf of stone.

The water turns passing faces,
innumerable pieces of silver.
I wash my hands, pack up, and
go home wishing I hadn't come.

Later, I eat my guilt.

EARLY MORNING FISHER

Stubbed at the pond's edge, blunted by his pipe,
his eyes are lined to the rod he strings and flails
through delicate arcs that flick the air with water.
Posing its own question, a swan sails
over its answers. Unconcerned, its mate
glides out from the rushes, shaping the breeze
that shifts the thin mist blenched from the back of darkness
to kindle dawn among the smoking trees.

Day broadens. The fisherman spreads his patience
angled only to tense and trap the bite
slashing the pond's translucence, sliver-knife
that flashes cold through cunning out of sight,
the pulse in that green-bottled ooze of life
each morning lairs afresh with a rocking light.

THESE TWO LOVERS

At any moment of the day
you'll suddenly turn to me and say:
'Tell me you love me.' So I do.
Yet, as I pass the words to you,
sometimes, preoccupied, my nuance
seems to deny you the assurance
you need so urgently. And I
find myself challenged to deny
the opposite of what I mean.
A sightless distance blurts between
us two, and I then re-discover
how islanded is loved from lover.

When all pretensions are unmade
and we together lie in bed
as lovers do, our bodies' act
renews the temporary pact
that shores a little warming grace
from the cold wash of nothingness.
But though you curl into my side,
fulfilled and sleepy, the divide
that mists us all, swirls back, and I
watch the Plough rust against the sky,
the sense of person and of place
sieved through the fall-away of space.

Until, unconsciously, you press
my hand against your nakedness.
Pulling me back to now and here,
you narrow distance from my fear.
I feel your breathing, and am sure
however torn or insecure
the lineaments of human trust,
our bodies' simple touching lust
tautens a wholeness running through
the variants of me and you,
so turn to sleep; like you, content
should this togetherness we're lent
prove to be all that living meant.

THIS BUSINESS OF LIVING

Midges fasten their mist-cloud over the river,
zizzing and zazzing, stitching intricacy,
an uncolliding shimmer, a pattern
that satisfies some midge necessity.

A wind, shuttling through roots of weeds and grasses,
side-slips against the weave of their symmetry
and breaks its shape. The rupture shifts, is mended,
then suddenly struck by a thrust of energy

the water twists up out of its element;
a kick of trout that heels midges from air,
recoiling under its own ripples, leaving
torn suspension, a gapped bite to repair.

Immediately the chromosomes reshuffle
to push the mist-cloud back to its old form,
and I, on the bank, experience satisfaction,
watching a small completeness assert its norm.

IN THE CHEVIOTS

A small black wedge, the shepherd
lets distance out of the hills,
turns and grunts at his dogs.
They knot up loops of space,
pulling sheep out of nowhere,
a flounce of waves that pour into
seething fanks of grey foam.

Coats of thick hill mist
trailed with tangled twigs and bracken
get peeled from stuck-out legs
one by one, and sheared strips
are stuffed in bags. Sheep, thinned
in a splashing yellow trough of bleat
from which they stagger, shake down
their hurt, diminished dignity
then, following their own baas, run
to where they left their nibbled journey.

The helpers' van fades through the valley
the dogs let space go free;
loosely the shepherd strolls home.
Distance re-inflates the hills.

A BALLAD OF ORPHEUS

On the third day after her unexpected death,
Orpheus descended into Hell.
It wasn't hard to find. He knew the directions well;
asleep, he'd often read them by the light of his own breath.

The doorkeeper was surly, but let him in;
he had no reason to keep anyone out.
Glaring like a lit city, a kind of visible shout
fungused about the place, an absolute din

of all notes, overtones and unheard sounds at once.
To keep his sense of self intact, he struck
a few familiar chords, and as his luck
would have it, she, who all along had felt a hunch

something unusual would happen, heard the order
and limiting purpose of his playing; and being not yet
fully subtracted out of herself to fit
Hell's edgeless ambiguities, broke from the border

of blurring dissolution, and moved towards her lover
as a cloud might move in the world of gods above.
He guessed that shape and stir to be his love
Eurydice, well knowing that no other

idea of woman would answer to the lyre
that sang against his loins. She came to him crying
aloud her numbed womanly tenderness, trying
to warm her cold half-body at the core of his fire.

But without a word said, he seized her hand
and began pulling her roughly along the road,
past the doorkeeper, who smirked, seeing the load
he carried. She, being woman, couldn't understand

that love in action needs no drag of speech,
and pled with him to turn round once and kiss
her. Of all the conditions the gods had imposed, this
was the one he dared not disobey. Reproach

followed reproach; till, as he fled
through shadow to shadow, suddenly it seemed
that the only absolute good was what he'd dreamed
of her. So Orpheus stopped, and slowly turned his head.

At once she began to small. He watched her disappear
backwards from him, and thought it best
that things should be so. How could he have stood the test
of constant loving, always with the fear

of his first loss ahead of him again,
believing happiness ends in boredom or pain?
So Orpheus returned by the same lane
as he went down by, to compose himself in a world of men.

SHETLAND PONY

A loose fold of steam idling
slumped in a roll of wet grass:
bridle in hand, me, soothing, sidling
up to its rest. One move to pass

the loop round its passivity,
and eyes clench, nostrils itch,
its breath flaring activity
as hocks and neck bend in a twitch

that plucks it up to throw a lunging
proud parabola. It shakes
the field's roots, and leaves me plunging
blundered angles out. It makes

knots in the wide circumference
of centuries it darkly flings
around that less old arrogance
by which my domination clings:

then suddenly trundle-bellies in
from what it's proved to where I stand
haltered in sweat; and, duty done,
nuzzles confinement from my hand.

GLASGOW NOCTURNE

Materialised from the flaked stones of buildings
dank with neglect and poverty, the pack,
thick-shouldered, slunk through rows of offices
squirting anonymous walls with their own lack

of self-identity. Tongs ya bass, Fleet,
Fuck the Pope spurted like blood: a smear
protesting to the passing daylight folk
the prowled-up edge of menace, the spoor of fear

that many waters cannot quench, or wash
clean from what hands, what eyes, from what hurt hearts?
O Lord! the preacher posed at the park gates,
what must we do to be whole in all our parts?

Late on Saturday night, when shop fronts doused
their furniture, contraceptives, clothes and shoes,
violence sneaked out in banded courage,
bored with hopelessness that has nothing to lose.

A side-street shadow eyed two lovers together;
he, lured from the loyalties of the gang
by a waif who wore her sex like a cheap trinket;
she, touched to her woman's need by his wrong

tenderness. On the way from their first dance,
the taste of not enough fumbled their search
of hands and lips endeared in a derelict close.
Over the flarepath of their love, a lurch

thrust from the shadow, circling their twined bodies.
It left them clung before its narrowing threat
till she shrieked. They peeled her from her lover,
a crumpled sob of a doll dropped in the street,

while he received his lesson: ribs and jaw
broken, kidneys and testicles ruptured, a slit
where the knife licked his groin. Before he died
in the ambulance, she'd vanished. Shops lit

up their furniture, contraceptives, clothes and shoes
again. Next morning, there was a darker stain
than Tongs ya bass and Fleet on the edge of the kerb;
but it disappeared in the afternoon rain.

ON A POSTCARD

*A postcard, posted in the reign of King Edward VII, has just
been delivered to the address for which it was intended. The
present occupant of the house has no knowledge of the person
to whom it was addressed. A post office spokesman said they*

had no idea why it had taken so long to reach its destination.
News item in a radio report.

Long skirts sweeping the sepia pavements; hats
like sitting birds with staring human faces;
cars creaked to their spokey wheels—a postcard
caught in a crack of sixty years ago,
flutters and lights on this destructive present;
an age that knew its places and its betters,
face upward with my morning's bills and letters.

The postures of these houses haven't changed
since that Edwardian summer when the weather
was 'simply grand', X marked the bedroom window
of someone's 'Loving Liz,' and all her loving
got poured into her postscript, 'wish you were here',
more X's breathing, 'Oh my dear, my dear!'

Wish you were here! Wind-hardened Roman soldiers
clinging their wall through stubborn Border hills
felt the same sap of warmth from Tuscany
soften the steeling cold their resolution
led them to strive to conquer life with swords,
until their Empire fell to these four words.

Wish you were here! How many sleepless pillows
have formed such troubled woman's balancings!
And yet fulfilment's what the mind makes bearable
as the flesh falls and faster fail the seasons,
till memory's the only harvest ripened
against what tenderness keeps men aware
that *There* is death, and *Here*'s not anywhere.

TWO GENERATIONS

A twig cracked, no louder than
a bone snapped in a furred trap.
Rabbits can't size fear. One flopped
across our harmless track slap

into the blue bolt a stoat
launched from a farm gate.
Fangs fastened the neck's shriek,
a cold killing without hate.

'Stop it,' the child cried: 'Oh, why don't you stop it?'
face to face with what has no stop,
and the useless pity that brought down
the back of my hand in a sharp chop.

GAMES MISTRESS

Always, and for its own sake, the game!
There was no other way for hopeful girls
to win their colours in the trials ahead
(necessarily unspecified beyond the
boundaries of school hymn and hockey pitch).
Generations careering towards this goal
coached from the side by her antiseptic figure,
upright as discipline, forwarding the game
that left her changeless on the cheering line.

Breath's taste in the kiss
against a hard-pressed door;
the steamed-up hand in the car
loosening motor senses;

the public bromide wedding
and honied harvestmoon;
legs arched for the trawl
of children out of birth;
the scarcely-noticed growth of
affection stronger than limbs;
cancer's surprise;
an ageing belly heaving
from dried-out opposite—

Fifty years backwards, through astonished tears,
some old girls gave her a silver hockey stick
with names of distinguished pupils carved upon it.
To this, of course, no game could be attached.

A CHRISTMAS CARD

Once more the old mythologies reassemble—
reindeer and angels canopy the city street
with lux aeterna while the clausing crowd's
cash-registered and carolled at supermarket heat.

Firs in tenement windows signature
in glittering cones of light the birth that needs no bed,
our public three-weeks' drying out of conscience
needling unhoovered carpets with their country spread.

Sceptics or sinners, none of us wise men,
for the most part aware that there's no beckoning star
to guide our possibilities, reflect
once more on where and what and why we think we are.

In this brief glow that warms our winter solstice
out of its ancient future-holding cold, our blood

reaches us towards its kind, and in rejoicing
preaches an incomplete and temporary good,
the raised glass pressure of our festive mood,
all that we know of it, or ever could.

ANON

They are excavating the mound at the foot of the village,
young men with gentle eyes and curious beards,
and names like Brown and Soutar, and soft-breasted girls
on whom they'll one day stamp their borrowed image,
name upon name. What else have they to preserve?

They are digging for signs. How like were the other Browns
and Soutars, ripening out of the nameless soil
and having to leave their names when it took them under?
Turning anonymity over and over,
they are finding only shards and pieces of bone.

THREE KINGS TALKING

After it was over, together in the sun,
three specialists in ruling, they compared
    notes, as farmers or carpenters might
warm to each other over the craft they shared.

One said: Although, of course, I'm no
believer in old wives' tales or popular rhymes,
    we have to take new situations
within the accepted context of the times.

For most, the times are never good,
as you both know. The idea of a saviour
    come as a babe caught peoples' fancy.
There seemed little chance of riotous behaviour

    over one so young, as long
as I fell in with their much-talked-of whim
    that what I had to do was follow
that strange, fast-moving star to come upon him.

The second said: Though it got you here,
we're all of us men of the world, and well aware
    that in the present state of knowledge
one can't account for what makes the simple stare.

The fact is, in my kingdom there was
unrest, dissatisfaction with the ruling line.
    Nothing you could single out;
unrest, a communal waiting for some sign

    that the heat and the flies and the shortage of food
they had to put up with—the sheer injustice of
    their lot—wasn't all that life
had to offer. I certainly don't mean to scoff

    at the kind of let-out this promised saviour
brings. If the gold, the frankincense and myrrh
    we've proffered in that stable buys us
relief from unrest, quells any possible stir

    a minority of dissidents might
have fanned up into open revolution,
    our journeys will have been worth while.
A child can't overthrow a constitution.

The third said: No doubt you're both right,
I don't think I'll forget that mother's face.
   A strange thing, too, the three of us
should come from the earth's ends to this untidy place

   we'd none of us heard of. Whatever the why
or the wherefore, we've done the sensible thing.
   If the child is holy, he'll be talked of
for longer than any politician or king.

   Let us keep silence over the reasons
each of us used to get here, and then go
   our ways, do what needs to be doing,
say what's expected of us, and who's to know

   of our understandable difficulties?
These three kings parted, each with his own rich train
   of satisfied diplomacy.
What happened next? They were never heard of again.

GIRL READING A LETTER

Clutching unopened a newly-delivered letter,
girl, sitting beside me in the bus,
full of too much, the flare of your breasts and the flush
of your crossed legs the lack of some man's delight;
how the ripe roundness, the soft unplucked promise
shrinks as your eyes pick withering from its pages,
and your body's stalked, as if for the first time,
by the gravity that pulls us all to the ground.

45

THE VACANT CHAIR

Suddenly, they broke out
of the discipline of absorbing facts
as if there really were such things.
Suddenly, they wanted to ask,
and have answered, the awkward questions.

Why scientists calculated
the cheapest form of total explosion?
Why children's bellies distended
with the needless obscenity of hunger?
Priests be permitted to father poverty
under the bedclothes of superstition?
Why those whom age had cataracted
with inoperable complacency
should profess to teach each generation
as if such blindness didn't exist?

A reasonable line was taken
by public and Press for a little while.
But at last they whom the blindness most
affected began to get angry. Who
were the young to expect answers for questions,
actions for needs? Why couldn't they stay
closed in their studies, leaving life
to settle at its own level,
accepting the absence of solutions?
After all, what they wanted
was, clearly, a Chair of Impossibilities.

And who could they have found to fill it?

ONE DAY AT SHIELDAIG

Behind rolled Vauxhall windows
two women, sealed in homely Aran sweaters,
knitted their fingers into sweated Arans.

Two men, cast off for
'a breath of air' (discreetly to water themselves),
came sweating back, two strolling Arans homing.

Even the clouds and mountains
got knitted up in patterns of each other,
the sea's fingers glinting incredibly.

TRAVELLING FOLK

Cornered in wastes of land, spinnies of old roads
lopped back from the new, where done horses
leant once on starved haunches, battered cars
nuzzle scrunted bushes and caravans.

Copper-breasted women suckle defiance
at schools inspectors. Sanitary men
are met with bronze-age scowls. All to no purpose.
Blown across Europe's centuries, bound only

in piths and withies to settlements not moved
by permanent impermanencies—smokey
violins, dusks gathered from skies
purple as hedge-fruits, or plucked stolen chickens—

These exiles from our human order seed
in the rough, overlooked verges of living,
their stubborn litter filling with vagrancy
the cracks our need for conformation shows.

GOD WOT

Mr. McCurdo wears long combinations.
In the business of life they mould his every step:
wool next the skin, continuing schoolboy comfort
for one who makes no move till he's 'done his prep'!

Mrs. McCurdo wears black camisoles
on a frequently measured pair of generous breasts
that helped to procure the best of marital bargains
for one whose buying's approved by consumer tests.

Combinations and camisoles hang in our garden,
blipped and flipped by the latest in washing machines;
placid, with all that was human rinsed out from them,
till suddenly there's a thumping like muffled screams:

McCurdo's legs break into a rage of dancing
while madam's bosom juts like a TV whore;
we think at our window: 'A lot of wind for the summer',
forget these two, look again, and then aren't sure.

Can such elegant, intimate, animal disguises
take fright at their wearers, chase after their own ends?
What else could washing contort and twist to escape from
but the human condition on which all washing depends?

AN ELEGY
(Matthew Lindsay: 1884–1969)

You might have died so many kinds of death
as you drove yourself through eighty-four Novembers—

1916. The Cameronian officer
keeping the Lewis gun he commanded chattering
over the seething mud, that the enemy
should be told only in terms of bulky bodies,
for which, oak leaves, a mention in dispatches.

1918. The fragment of a shell
leaving one side of a jaw and no speech,
the bone graft from the hip. Shakespeare mouthed
(most of the others asserting silences)
over and over again, till the old words
shaped themselves into audibility.

1921. An eighty-per-cent
disability pension, fifty the limit of life
expectancy, a determination of courage
that framed the public man, the ready maker
of witty dinner speeches, the League of Nations,
the benefits of insurance, the private man
shut in his nightly study, unapproachable,
sufficient leader of sporting tournaments,
debates, and the placing of goodwill greetings in clubs.

1935. Now safely past
the doctors' prophecies. Four children, a popular
outward man wearing maturity,
top of his business tree, when the sap falters
and the soon-to-be again confounded doctors
pronounce a world-wide cruise the only hope,
not knowing hope was all he ever needed
or counted on to have to reckon with.

1940 to 50. Wartime fears
not for himself but for his family,
the public disappointments and the private

disasters written off with stock quotations
from Shakespeare or Fitzgerald, perhaps to prove
the well-known commonness of experience,
the enemy across the mud, old age.

1959. It was necessary
at seventy-five, to show he couldn't be taken
by enfilading weaknesses. A horse
raised his defiance up. It threw him merely
to Russia on a stretcher, with two sticks
to lean beginner's Russian upon.

1969. The end of a decade
of surgeons, paling blindness, heart attacks
all beaten with familiar literature
bent into philosophic platitudes,
to the January day in his dressing-gown
when he sat recording plans for a last Burns Supper—

You might have died so many kinds of death
as you drove yourself through eighty-four Novembers
till you fell from your bed, apologised for such foolishness,
and from your sleep rode out where no man goes.

CERTAIN KILLERS

You'd think a mouse so mere a thing
it shouldn't be too hard to kill.

Men believe it crumbs germs
from daily swept-under boards;
women shriek up chairs for fear
it runs against their privacies.

I laid a baited trap. By night
the sprung bar pushed eyes
out of the crushed head. By day
blood ran down disposable whiskers.

I could, of course, keep a cat
to eat my scraps of chopped meat;
but I like birds—they keep their distance—
and cats think all cheeps
signal their pounce of destruction.
Besides, I don't think I could stand
being contempt's glared target
for not doing my own small murders.

A CHANGE OF FASHION

On Summer holidays
my trouser turn-ups collected grains of sand,
pieces of shells and other memorabilia.

On earning days
I'd brush out these dried sights of sea and sky
to make way for the hairs of casual carpets.

You can't gather
capsuled space in trousers;
so now we've done away with turn-ups, and are
becoming less familiar with ourselves.

SAILORS' QUARTER, AMSTERDAM

His eyes met hers. Like to come in? they asked.
How much? He nodded. Price fixed, he followed her
into a room darkened with coolness, and took off
embarrassed trousers. You must wear this, she said,
to keep me clean, the nurse-like fingers moving
adroitly. Only the Spanish gentlemen won't
because of their religion. Ah! a good one
you have there. We'll have fun together.
Help me undress.

            The hooks of her tight bodice
thickened the pluck of his fingers. Apples on their tree,
the soft mouth of persuasion, silently spoke
the risen serpent, blood blurting to blood,
that first unloosened Eden's mythic flood.

Time became touch as, agelessly beneath,
she bucked him down to the emptied present. He got off
to meet it. Are you a local girl?
The season good for tourists? Had fine weather?
he asked, adjusting his dress before leaving.
School-marm comforting little boy, she patted
him on the head of his conversational strain,
shook hands, re-locked her apartment door, and left him,
his rub of fever chafered to the bone,
beside the gut of a canal, alone.

SATURDAY AFTERNOON

She tries on different hats,
unruffles to the mirror's eye

as if each topping whorl of colour
its vacant gaze lit on, might help
her slant herself a new meaning,
perhaps even an old meaning
that somewhere lay about half-shaped
like hats forgotten, dusty cloth.

He sits there bored, a shabby peacock,
the tawdry feathers of his mind
lifting him nowhere; twentieth-century
man dumped on his disillusions,
knowing hats make no difference,
eyeing up girls with listless lust,
jarred by their bright and eager chatter;
wondering what it is they hope for.

A MASS OF MOZART'S

Rococo angels chuff their puffy cheeks;
filigree sunshine filters cream and gold
through sainted windows: consolation gleams,
unquestionable as authority;
a sensuous arras hangs, and flames of candles
lean to it, breathing out their soft hosannas.

Agnus dei, who took away the sins
of the eighteenth-century world where Mozart poured
his order and assurance through these words
worn smooth by Latin centuries, for me,
Kyrie eleison, sceptic shadows lie
along the mind's cold crevices. The chill of faithful
stone that has outlived its common purpose
no longer shields to bless. Yet the unanswerable

Dona nobis pacem soars above
these gilded prayers, those rafters of belief;
and though no heaven holds the judgment winds'
four corners, and the old imagined earth
turns aimless, there's at least the heart's *Amen*
that music moulds such certain transiencies.

FEELING SMALL

The coldest day for thirty years.

Scuffed among the stained snow
of petrol pumps, a thrush hung out
its broken wing, the grounded eyes
glazed with a finishing of fear.
Before long, I thought, a car
will crunch it quickly, or someone else
snap its neck against a stone.
I turned away, reproaching myself
for wasting pity on a small bird,
so much that's larger claiming pity.

It had gone when I got back,
cleanly, without blood or feathers.
I was able to drive home
to dinner, television news
from which all essences of pity
had been most carefully extracted;
make good my warm accustomed loves.

The coldest day for thirty years.

NAMELESS

You step from underthings,
lie down beside me.
What we touch is earth
parched with explanation.

Rain over Eden
feels its way across us.
Trembling, it spills
unexplained release.

THE CLUB

Around the lunched togetherness of the world
he'd left, the grounds of his spirit shored him up
when the decade-younger generations called him
by his first name; each stirred coffee cup
remembering how once he'd played a part
in the rise and fall of unpredictable pressures.
Industrious barometer, his heart
had given out. But now that he'd the leisure
to do the things he wanted, he looked fitter
than he had done for years. You'll see fourscore
at least, their laid-down saucers clattered. Later,
the last of them extracted through the door
swung on the gloss of business, a leather chair
snoozed him from staring out on nothing at all
where, waivering his final blue-chip share,
he'd wonder at what bidding death might call.

SUBJECTIVE PROJECTIVE

amber
slow up
red red—

clicky clack clack domenico scarlatti
open the window
breathe fresh pollution
quite a belly that girl's carrying
wonder if she got it in bed
or in the back of some man's car
defending women's right to freedom
whatever the christ that is—

did he spit down that drain
just because the drain was there
gaping up at him
god
the permissive society—

hairy enough to be a poet
too damn many of them
any bugger can be a poet
now that you can't nail thoughts with rhyme
or even have thoughts
too oldfashioned for collapsing society
the sunday critics cry
wishing they could write poems themselves
probably why they cry—

girls get pregnant
men spit down drains
poems aren't so very different—

red domenico
ruffled cock in spanish courtyard
who the hell cares anyway—

art for art's sake
drains for drains' sake
girls for producing girls for producing girls for—

green green
go go go
i accelerate you accelerate they accelerate
we move forward

THE ARRIVAL

Sickened by fumes and futile argument,
I crossed the ritualled boundary of week's end
to sit beside a burn; the dank earth-scent
it rose from held against each rucked-up bend
of water balancing within some twist
of the wind's hand the unity I missed.

Beyond a broken fence dropped to a cross
a lark hoisted its clarity, topping sight
with the sharp edge of its sound; a weightless loss
of dusty feathers shearing flakes of light
to visible singing, hung above the grassed
and dappled cows, each in its own plashed shadow massed.

And I who, tired with the run of the city's day,
sought earth's healing last word, apprehended
continual becoming; nature's say

the lark-spun air, torn water endlessly mended,
the wind's wrist affirming perpetual change
to us who are the rhythm, not the range.

FRUITS

She rolled the Easter egg of her belly
through the pinging-open door
to lean her turn against the earth
smell of vegetables. As he rung
the till on chatter of last night's telly,
he noticed stains like sour sapples,
detergent hands, bare legs veined
blue by seven kids in as many
years. Eve with all her Eden drained,
she shook out her last penny.
He handed her back bruised apples.

GONE FOR A SONG

A canvas booth in a passing market-place;
a thumb-stained vocal score of Handel's *Messiah*
salted by mould's invasions and erosions;
the date, eighteen seventy-six; the price,
twenty-five pence. Between the unplotted pock-marks
paper gets foxed with, earthing towards corruption
a spidery hand still pointed its assertion:
Miss Langston loves the music of G. F. Handel.

She knew that her redeemer lived while her father,
a breathless bull, roared twenty widowed winters,
cowing her mien with iron-mastered money,
the rage of his beard swelling the roped veins
of his head whenever a likely man so much
as pondered what her draperies concealed.

Always the music of G. F. Handel healed
the stripes of her wasted womanhood
as tea tinkled and silvery scones
wore the sun from talked-out Empire skies.

Women with silent lips shot out their scorn
at the likes of her, whom no respected husband
filled and refilled with children; whose thin breasts
were never stirred except to apprehension
of some imagined cancer.

Death smelted the master's iron strength
back to the loam from which his ore was won,
leaving her emptiness;
the ravelled, broken strains of middle-age,
like sheep astray. Aware that everything
cries help to nothing, none to hear or blame—
leaves on the window-pane fluttering, grass
wavering, breath more difficult now
on stairs and in crescendos—still his music
filled the increasing cracks that words and moments
levered half-open, softened the brash glare
that surfaced each new day. In gratitude
for these unspeakable comforts, the sharp pen
crawled on its page: *Miss Langston loves the music
of G. F. Handel*, one chorused heart's *Amen*.

PLACE DE LA CONTR' ESCARPE

Walking through hours of narrow streets
in Miller's and Hemingway's Paris, we reached a square
enclosed by centuries sagged against each other:
homes that had stared out the Terror,
the Commune, Hitler, the rising of 'Sixty Eight.

In the tallest building a window suddenly opened,
a dark girl leant out and stayed there, singing;
not noticed by the women hobbling beneath
their endless concern with how to make ends meet,
the students strolling arm-in-arm between
fresh lunges at sex, or arguing
interminably over coffee the bombs
of Vietnam, rank black injustices,
what others' lives their words could use to wrench
from humankind its frailty and strangeness.

CALLANISH

Two dwindling lovers run to the Standing Stones:
she, leaning against a slab's root, her full
breasts humping a cheap summer frock;
he, crouching to fill his camera-spool
with the novelty of her smile. A wind to the sea spoke,
shifting the loose weight from its sandy bones.

Safe enough now to pose in this rattled jaw
decay has weathered open; idly to prise
sheep droppings, birds' feathers, a rabbit skull aside
from teeth stumped blunt by want of sacrifice,

60

Earth having now more varied deaths to bride.
Once, an expectant breath of people saw

blindfolded boys and virgins forced to lean
bared throats to waiting vessels; felt the scream
fix to each draining face, their heated blood
invoke dark sleep from seed and semen, teem
with sap whatever multiplied, make good
thin fields and beasts' and women's wombs, between

one hunger and the next. The lovers rise, move off,
unnoticed minutes from their slip of time
dripped to the rimless vessel of what's passed
that chills all human blood; only the rime
of silence against silence left at last
to distance and the shrugging sea's cough.

THE DEVIL'S ELBOW

Driving northwards through the dusk,
the car lights were blocked by banks of mist
exhaling thyme and heather. They'd unbent
another hairpin when the wire of the road
was suddenly furred with rabbits. Swerve or brake,
you couldn't avoid them. You could only sense
the unprotesting burst of their bodies.

Stop it! I hate you! For Christ's sake stop it!,
the girl in the passenger seat cried,
as if it was someone's fault; as if one could simply
stop at half-way nowhere. The wheels turned off
the small stains. A singer of heroic
suffering, of deaths larger than life,
sat sobbing in the steady purr of the car
taking her to the place of her next engagement.

SEEN OUT

Over small print in papers,
arguments at Public Inquiries,
a demolition squad moves in;
coloured helmets swarming up to
patched roofs, unpicking rafters,
levering slabs through ceilings,
gulping cupboards sheer with air.

Now and then a tenement
fights back, stumps snarling
chokes of dust, menacing
what once had been a passing street.
Machines bring all stone
down to its own level.

On a half-cleared site where soon
rows of red and yellow curtains
would be switched-on stacks of light,
I found the handle of a pan,
a mattress spring, a chair's leg,
the bric-a-brac of done-with caring;
while from one grey isolated
tenement storey, with cushions,
blandishments and blankets
they prised loose an old woman
from a sense of place that hadn't
quite seen out her time.

AN OCCASION

A heart attack, the papers said.
I sat in the crematorium chapel,

watching mourners not quite sure
how best look solemn or work prayer,
and realised not one strained face
was known to me. But it was now
too late, or early, to get out.

The coffin looked like other coffins
humped beneath a velvet cloth.
The minister, hired out like clothes
for some unnatural occasion,
intoned what he was there to say,
then read a filial eulogy
type-written with a key missing.

Instead of paying last respects
to a professor of philosophy,
I sat there listening to how well
a wholesale grocer of the name
had played his part. Nice you could come,
the relatives remarked through tears.

I murmured the condolences
I mothball with my black coat—
they're suitable for every man—
then stood outside a moment, watching
strangers, troubled briefly, disappear:
anonymous smoke signing anonymous air.

BLOW-UP

They led the leader out to his execution
wearing a hat against the heat of the sun.
He stood backed to a wall wearing the hat,
the flush of unappreciated efforts

on behalf of his people, and (of course) himself,
drained from his bandaged face. At a given signal
a row of rifles spurted, the hat jumped
clean into the air, a fat body
shrunk; a cheer ballooned, coloured with windy
slogans, airs of humanity and justice.
Soldiers tossed a body onto a truck;
humanity and justice thinned, deflated
for the time being, leaving behind a pool
of blood, a hat upturned to the sun.

TOWARD LIGHT

The distant fog-horns bicker, the near ones boom;
light bats across the ceiling of the room
where, forty years ago, I watched, awake;
a still unfocused schoolboy trying to take
life by the meaning. Then, the mist that gripped
the perfumed garden, kept the sea tight-lipped,
hung vague on sheltering curtains; the boy's mind
compassed on ships whose fogs lay far behind.
Now, with the frame loose, the window bare,
a blunt beam's thrown back on its own stare.